You Can Go to the Potty

William Sears, M.D., Martha Sears, R.N.,
and Christie Watts Kelly

Illustrated by Renée Andriani

Little, Brown and Company ❧ Boston New York London

To the many toilet learners in Dr. Bill's practice who've "done it themselves"
proudly when the time was right
— *W. S.* and M. S.

To the University of Memphis Barbara K. Lipman Early Childhood
School and Research Institute, for consistently demonstrating loving and
developmentally appropriate practices in teaching children
— C. W. K.

For Jillian, with love
— R. A.

Text copyright © 2002 by William Sears, Martha Sears, and Christie Watts Kelly
Illustrations copyright © 2002 by Renée Andriani

First Edition

Library of Congress Cataloging-in-Publication Data

Sears, William, M.D.
    You can go to the potty / William Sears, Martha Sears, and Christie Watts Kelly ; illustrated by Renée
Andriani. — 1st ed.
        p. cm.
    Summary: A guide for parents and children to use for toilet training.
    ISBN 0-316-78888-0
    1. Toilet training — Juvenile literature. 2. Children — Health and hygiene — Juvenile literature. 3. Children — Care — Juvenile literature. [1. Toilet
training.] I. Sears, Martha. II. Kelly, Christie Watts. III. Andriani, Renée, ill. IV. Title.

RJ61 .S44194 2002
649'.62 — dc21   2001038113

10 9 8 7 6 5 4 3 2 1

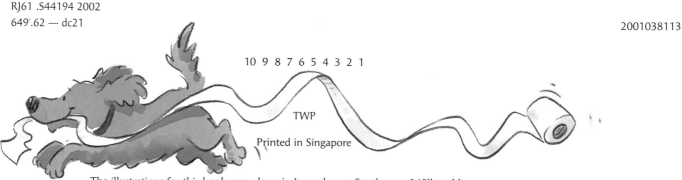

TWP

Printed in Singapore

The illustrations for this book were done in Lumadye on Strathmore 140lb. cold press paper.
The text was set in Joanna and Angie, and the display type is Forte MT.

NOTES FOR PARENTS AND CAREGIVERS

Parents and caregivers will find it helpful to read these notes and preview this book before sharing it with a child. The text and illustrations reflect a responsive parenting style known as Attachment Parenting. (See "About Attachment Parenting" on page 32.)

❧ We may think in terms of "potty training" or "potty teaching" our child, but from a child's point of view it is "potty *learning.*"

❧ A potty-learning child will generally start with a readiness period, first becoming aware of toileting through observing and talking about it with others. During this time the child may be able to verbalize *after the fact* that a diaper is full. When the child is able to verbalize it *before the fact,* many families enter a more proactive phase in which the child is encouraged to use the potty but still wears diapers. Finally, when the child is able to stay clean and dry most of the time, the child graduates to training pants or underwear and can do many of the toileting steps independently. Depending upon the temperaments of the child and the parents, this process can last anywhere from two days to two years or more. Children vary widely in the ages at which they completely master potty learning. Watch for a typical sequence of mastery: nighttime bowel control, daytime bowel control, daytime bladder control, nighttime bladder control.

❧ Some children, especially boys, may continue to be wet at night long after having complete daytime control. If your child reaches six years old and is still wet almost nightly, seek medical advice.

❧ Timing is everything when it comes to starting the proactive phase of potty learning. The child must be not only physically and mentally ready, but emotionally ready as well. Young children tend to go through cycles of development in which they're receptive to new things for a period of time and then negative about new things for a period of time. If you catch your child in a negative phase, you'll set yourself up for a power struggle. Big events such as bringing home a new baby, moving, starting preschool, and so on, can induce a negative phase for a child.

A parent who has been attuned to a child's needs since birth is more likely to sense the appropriate time to begin actively teaching toilet skills. Some physical readiness signs include the child's ability to stay dry for up to three hours at a time, pull pants up and down, and display "about to go" signals (verbalizing, grabbing at the front of a diaper, squatting, or going to a private place such as behind the couch or in a closet). Mental readiness signs include the ability to understand and respond to simple instructions, the ability to communicate bodily sensations such as hunger or thirst, and simply showing interest in the potty.

Modeling is the best way to teach toilet skills. When your toddler accompanies you to the bathroom "classroom," describe each step you're going through: "I'm pulling down my pants. I'm sitting on the potty. I'm letting the 'pee-pee' or 'poo-poo' come out. I'm wiping (can you hand me some toilet paper?). I'm standing up. I'm pulling my pants up. I'm flushing (would you like to flush the potty for me?). I'm washing my hands."

Model good hygiene as well. Let your child see you washing your hands with soap and water each time you use the toilet. Help your toddler make the connection by washing your and your toddler's hands after each diaper change.

Some children are afraid of flushing, either because of the noise or because they are afraid to see a "part of themselves" disappear. After you've gone to the bathroom, let your child peer over the edge of the toilet and look at your "production," then help you flush it down so it is seen as a natural part of the event. Some children are even afraid to put their own "production" in the potty or toilet, preferring to deposit it in the familiar diaper. If your child has that problem, try an intermediate step of laying a clean diaper across the seat of the potty and allowing your child to use it that way for a while.

Show a girl how to wipe in one front-to-back motion when she urinates, and to reach around behind but still wipe in a front-to-back motion for BMs. Explain that "this will keep your poo-poo away from your vulva [or vagina] so you won't get sore." To ensure cleanliness when it comes to BMs, parents will need to assist both boys and girls with wiping for a couple more years.

Boys require additional instruction because of their anatomy. It is easiest to teach a boy to urinate sitting, holding his penis down to direct the flow of urine into the potty (for a young learner, a parent can hold the penis down at first until the child picks up the skill). Learning this way also replaces the need for a urine deflector, which can sometimes hinder or even injure a child. Daddy or a potty-trained peer can demonstrate how to sit on the toilet and point the penis down. When a potty chair or adapter seat for the toilet isn't available, both boys and girls can sit facing backward on a regular toilet to avoid the feeling that they're falling in, and this will also help a boy's penis point down. Later, provide opportunities for boys to see their father and their peers standing up to urinate. When they are beginning to practice this new skill, homemade or store-bought tissue-paper "targets" that float on the surface of the water can be very helpful in improving aim.

🖐 Don't let little feet dangle! It's important for children's feet to be planted on the floor or a firm surface so they can relax the muscles involved in urination and defecation (which we call the "doughnut" muscles). To this end, potty chairs are better than a seat that fits on an adult toilet, unless the adult toilet is equipped with a step stool on which the child can firmly plant his or her feet.

🖐 Just as you would never punish a child learning to walk for falling down, you should never punish your child for any aspect of learning to use the potty. For example, when urine gets on the toilet seat or floor, calmly have your child wipe it up with tissue.

🖐 Positive reinforcement (praise, stickers, treats,

and so on) can be appropriate, but avoid giving your child the message that his or her worth depends on performance.

🖐 Some children think of urinating and defecating as pleasurable sensations they want to "hoard" to themselves. This may make them reluctant to tell you when they need to go because they feel you'll interrupt this process.

🖐 On the other hand, children who have had a painful bowel movement due to constipation can be so afraid of experiencing pain again that they hold back. They can become impacted and create a vicious cycle that may lead to the need for suppositories or even an enema (never administer these without medical advice). If your child has been constipated with no BMs in three or four days, seek medical advice. The best prevention for constipation is to drink plenty of fluids (at least four cups a day for children) and eat plenty of fiber from sources such as fresh fruits and vegetables.

🖐 We have chosen commonly used words that will be familiar to most families to describe the toileting process, but of course you can substitute other words used by your family. The "Answers for the Very Curious" sidebars will give you additional technical and child-friendly language to explain body parts and functions involved in toileting.

When you were a baby, you needed *lots* of help from Mommy and Daddy. You needed help eating — so you were given special milk and baby food.

You needed help sleeping —
so you were rocked and patted and held closely.

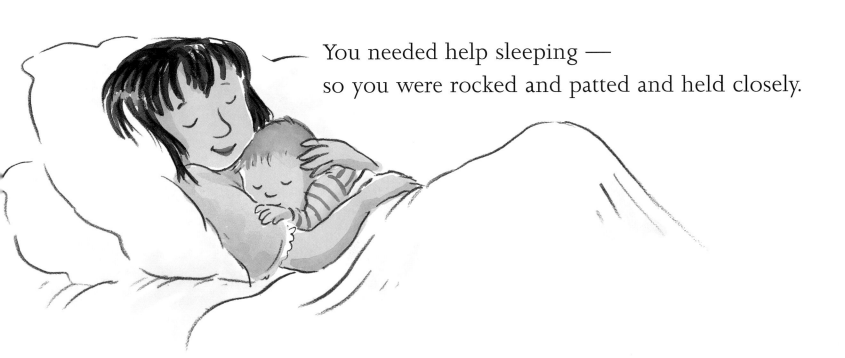

You needed help staying warm and comfy —
so you were dressed in soft clothes
and a clean, dry diaper.

7

Babies can't talk, so they cry.
You cried, too.

You cried when you were hungry . . .

when you were sleepy . . .

and even when your diaper was
full of pee-pee or poo-poo.

Whenever you cried, Mommy and Daddy
helped you feel better.

Now you're getting older. You can do
more and more things each day.

When you're hungry, you can say,
"Food, please," and Mommy or Daddy
will get you something to eat.

When you're sleepy, you might
crawl right into bed,
and they will tuck you in.

When your diaper is full of pee-pee or poo-poo, you can tell
Mommy or Daddy, and they will give you a clean, dry diaper.

If your diaper has poo-poo in it, they might empty it into the toilet and flush it down. Poo-poo goes bye-bye in the toilet. That's where it belongs. Pee-pee belongs there, too.

All grown-ups and older kids
put their pee-pee and poo-poo
right into the toilet,
without using a diaper.

Growing-up kids like you can put their pee-pee and poo-poo into a little potty. Or they might even use a big toilet.

You can watch Mommy and Daddy and older kids to see how to go to the potty. You can hand them toilet paper so they can wipe their bottoms clean. You can flush the toilet for them. You can remind them to wash their hands.

Answers for the Very Curious

🐾 Why do boys have a penis and girls have a vulva and vagina? Because boys' and girls' bodies are made differently. Boys will grow up to be like Daddy, and girls will grow up to be like Mommy.

You will keep wearing diapers until you learn how to notice that pee-pee and poo-poo are ready to come out.

When you feel the pee-pee coming, just say, "Go pee-pee!"

When you feel the poo-poo coming, just say, "Go poo-poo!"

And Mommy or Daddy will take you to the potty.

When you can keep your diapers clean and dry most of the time, you will be ready to wear special big-kid underpants instead of a diaper. You can pick out the ones you like the best.

WHAT YOU CAN DO

❧ Visit the store with Mommy or Daddy and help pick out a potty.

❧ Help choose special big-kid underpants.

❧ Invite a friend over who already knows how to go to the potty.

21

Then, when you feel the pee-pee or poo-poo might be coming, you can say, "I need to go to the potty!"

And run to the potty all by yourself...

pull down your
big-kid underpants . . .

sit on the potty . . .
and let the pee-pee
or poo-poo come out.

You will still need a little help from Mommy or Daddy
to wipe your bottom clean, pull up your pants,
empty your pee-pee or poo-poo into the big toilet,
flush it down, and wash your hands.

WHAT YOU CAN DO

❧ Practice pulling your pants and underpants up and down by yourself.

❧ Practice wiping a baby doll. Later you can wipe yourself when you use the potty. Always wipe front to back. Get help from an adult when you have a poo-poo.

❧ Practice emptying your potty into the big toilet, with help.

Sometimes you might sit on the potty and wait and wait and wait.
But no pee-pee or poo-poo comes out.
That's okay. You can try again later.

ANSWERS FOR THE VERY CURIOUS

🐛 Where does pee-pee come out? A girl has a little opening (urethra) in the front of her bottom (vulva), and a boy has a little opening (urethra) in his penis, where the pee-pee (urine) comes out.

🐛 Where does poo-poo come out? Girls and boys have another opening (anus) in their bottoms where the poo-poo (stool) comes out.

🐛 How do I get my pee-pee and poo-poo to stay in or come out? A muscle shaped like a doughnut is around each opening. You can squeeze it shut to keep the pee-pee or poo-poo in, or make it open up to let it out.

🐛 Why won't my poo-poo come out? Sometimes you can get constipated (your poo-poo is hard and big, and pushing it out might hurt). Drink lots of water and eat lots of fruits and vegetables to make your poo-poo softer.

Sometimes the pee-pee or poo-poo will come out too fast, before you can get to the potty. Oops! That's okay, too. If it's pee-pee, you can help clean it up. If it's poo-poo, Mommy or Daddy will clean it up for you.

Sometimes you might still wear diapers at nap time, or bedtime, or when you go places, even if you already know how to go to the potty. And that's okay, too. Soon you will be clean and dry all the time, and you'll wear big-kid underpants all the time, too.

ANSWERS FOR THE
VERY CURIOUS

Why do I have pee-pee accidents? Some kids have smaller bladders (the little "balloon" where the pee-pee collects in your body). Some kids have trouble holding it in. Sometimes during the day you're so busy you forget to go to the potty. And at night, you're so sleepy it's hard to wake up.

When you were a baby, you needed Mommy and Daddy to do *everything* for you. Now that you're growing up, you are learning to do all kinds of things by yourself — eating, getting dressed, and even going to the potty.

Mommy and Daddy are very proud of you.
They are still there to help you whenever you need it,
and they love you more and more each day.

About Attachment Parenting

Attachment parenting is a *responsive* style of parenting that helps facilitate a child's secure emotional attachments. When parents understand, anticipate, and meet their children's needs in a developmentally appropriate way, they establish a warm, connected relationship based on love and trust.

Connectedness, love, and *trust* — but not permissiveness — are keys to the attachment parenting concept of discipline. When parents model desirable behavior and set boundaries and consequences based on a child's readiness, children tend to behave appropriately out of a desire to please rather than the fear of punishment.

Attachment parenting is an *approach,* rather than a strict set of rules. It's the way many people parent instinctively — comforting a crying baby, showing an older child a constructive way to vent frustrations, guiding children to independence by providing a secure base. The following "Five Baby Bs" are attachment parenting tools that can help parents and babies get connected right from the start.

1. Birth bonding: Babies need to continue feeling connected after birth, no matter what kind of birth situation. Planning ahead to allow skin-to-skin contact with mom and dad, breastfeeding, and rooming-in with your baby if at the hospital will set the stage for a good start to the parenting relationship.

2. Breastfeeding: Human milk is the best food for baby humans. Breastfeeding as soon as possible after birth gives the optimal chance for a good start. Continuing as long as possible helps both baby and parents reap the most benefits.

3. Babywearing: Carried babies are more content and less fussy, giving them more quiet and alert time for cognitive and physical development. Being physically close to baby helps parents learn to read baby's signals and develop intuition about baby's needs.

4. Bedding close to baby: Babies need to be close to parents at night as well as during the daytime. Co-sleeping (sleeping in the same bed or the same room) can be an effective way to satisfy a baby's needs as well as to make life easier for a nursing mother. It also helps working parents reconnect with their children after being separated all day.

5. Belief in the language value of a baby's cry (and other cues): Since infants can't talk, their only means of communication are through body language and crying. Parents learn to read their baby's body language and pre-cry signals as well as their cries and respond appropriately to the baby's needs, helping baby develop trust and communication skills.

Resources

www.askdrsears.com is an interactive Web site where you can ask — and find the answers to — your toughest parenting questions.

www.parenting.com features articles by and chats and workshops with William and Martha Sears.

The Sears Children's Library, by William Sears, M.D., Martha Sears, R.N., and Christie Watts Kelly, and illustrated by Renée Andriani
Baby on the Way
What Baby Needs
Eat Healthy, Feel Great

The Sears Parenting Library, by William Sears, M.D., and Martha Sears, R.N.
The Attachment Parenting Book: A Commonsense Guide to Understanding and Nurturing Your Baby
The Pregnancy Book: Everything You Need to Know from America's Baby Experts, written with Linda Hughey Holt, M.D., F.A.C.O.G.
The Birth Book: Everything You Need to Know to Have a Safe and Satisfying Birth
The Breastfeeding Book: Everything You Need to Know About Nursing Your Child From Birth Through Weaning
The Baby Book: Everything You Need to Know About Your Baby — From Birth to Age Two
The Fussy Baby Book: Everything You Need to Know — From Birth to Age Five
The Discipline Book: Everything You Need to Know to Have a Better-Behaved Child — From Birth to Age Ten
The Family Nutrition Book: Everything You Need to Know About Feeding Your Children — From Birth Through Adolescence
The A.D.D. Book: New Understandings, New Approaches to Parenting Your Child, written with Lynda Thompson, Ph.D.

Attachment Parenting International (API) is a member organization networking with attachment parents, professionals, and like-minded organizations around the world. In addition to parent support groups, the organization provides educational and research materials. 1508 Clairmont Place, Nashville, TN 37215, USA; www.attachmentparenting.org; 615-298-4334.

La Leche League International (LLLI) is the world's foremost authority on breastfeeding, offering breastfeeding support groups, lifelong nutrition advice, one-on-one help for breastfeeding mothers, and a catalog of products and literature. 1400 North Meacham Road, Schaumburg, IL 60173-4048, USA; www.lalecheleague.org; 847-519-7730; 800-LA-LECHE (525-3243).